# ALL ABOUT ME:

MY NAME IS

PHOTO

MY FAVOURITES

MY DISLIKES

CONTENTS

Starter....About us

Have got
There is and there are
prepositions of place

My name's Jamie, I'm seven
This is my dad 1
This is my mum 2
This is my grandpa 3
This is my grandma 4
This is my uncle 5
This is my aunt 6
This is my cousin , his is name is Brian 7
This is my sister 8
she's got long black hair

Starter.... About us

> We use *have got* to say that someone has or owns something. We also use *have got* to say how people and things look

Affirmative			Negative	
Short form	Long form		Short form	Long form
I´ve got	I have got		I haven't got	I have not got
he´s got	he has got		he hasn't got	he has not got
she´s got	she has got		she hasn't got	she has not got
it´s got	it has got		it hasn't got	it has not got

1. Complete the sentences

She´s got   He´s got   I´ve got

1. I´ve got black hair, but _____ brown hair

2. This is Alison _____ red hair . This Claire _____ blonde hair

3. This is Andy _____ short hair . This Diane _____ long hair

4. This is my uncle _____ straight hair . This aunt _____ wavy hair

Starter.... About us

2. Write the words in the correct order. Then match

1. He´s got hair light brown

He´s got light brown hair
_____

2. Shes´s blonde got hair

_____

3. got He´s hair brown dark

_____

4. black got She´s hair

_____

5. long hair got She´s

_____

6. hair curly got She´s

_____

Starter.... About us

3. Make the sentences negative

1. He´s got brown hair. _____

2. She´s got long hair. _____

3. I´ve got short hair _____

4. He´s got curly hair. _____

5. She´s got blonde hair. _____

6. he´s got straight hair. _____

Starter.... About us

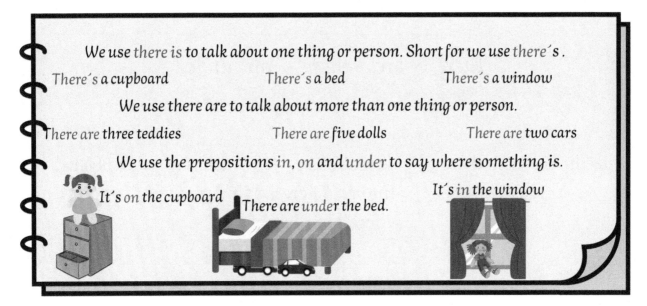

We use there is to talk about one thing or person. Short for we use there's.

There's a cupboard   There's a bed   There's a window

We use there are to talk about more than one thing or person.

There are three teddies   There are five dolls   There are two cars

We use the prepositions in, on and under to say where something is.

It's on the cupboard   There are under the bed.   It's in the window

Starter.... About us

4. Look at the picture and write T or F

1. There are three teddies on the bed.   _ _ _ _ _ _ _ _ _

2. There's a ball under the window.   _ _ _ _ _ _ _ _ _

3. There's a car under the bed.   _ _ _ _ _ _ _ _ _

4. There are three dolls in the room.   _ _ _ _ _ _ _ _ _

5. Look at the picture and complete the description.

there   are   there's   on   under

In the bedroom there _ _ _ _ _ five dolls. _ _ _ _ _ _ a bed and a cupboard. _ _ _ _ _ _ are two cars _ _ _ _ _ the bed. There are three teddies _ _ the bed and there's one ball

Unit 1 My feelings

The verb be

I'm happy
He's hot
She's tired

We use the verb be with adjectives that describe how we feel

short forms	long forms	adjectives
I'm	i am	
you're	you are	hot cold
he's	he is	sad happy
she's	she is	thirsty brave
it's	it is	hungry scared
we're	we are	angry tired
you're	you are	
they're	they are	

Unit 1. My feelings

1. Circle the forms of *be*

This (is) my classroom.
These are my friends.
They´re happy.
I´m happy too. We´re happy

2. Match

1. We´re happy   __

2. He´s angry   __

3. She´s thirsty   __

4. You´re sad   __

5. I´m hungry   __

A   B   C

D   E

   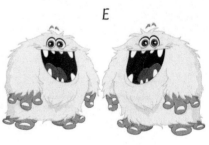

Unit 1. My feelings

3. Write the short forms of *be*.

´s   ´re   ´m

That´s Ted, he´s tired . And that's Tina she__ thirsty. Look at Holly and Hannah they__ happy. I can see Sam he__ sad and Arthur he__ angry. I__ Henry and this is Harry and we__ hungry

4. Write sentences. Use *happy* 😁 or *sad* ☹

1. 😁 I _____

2. 😁😁 We _____

3. ☹ You _____

4. ☹ He _____

5. 😁 She _____

6. ☹☹ They _____

Unit 1. My feelings

Questions with *be*

We can use *be* to ask yes/no questions. We change the word order in questions

	Statement	Question
	She´s sad.	Is she sad?

Question	Short answers, positive	Answer negative
Am I __?	Yes, I am.	No, I´m not.
Are you __?	Yes, you are.	No, you aren't
Is he __?	Yes, he is.	No, he isn't.
Is she __?	Yes, she is.	No, she isn't.
Is it __?	Yes, it is.	No, it isn't.
Are we __?	Yes, we are	No, we aren't
Are you __?	Yes, you are.	No, you aren't.
Are they __?	Yes , they are.	No, they aren't.

Unit 1. My feelings

5. Write the correct form of *be*.

1. Is he sad?   Yes _____

2. Are they happy?   Yes _____

3. Is she hungry??   No _____

4. Are they thirsty?   No _____

6. Write questions.

1. I´m tired   _____

2. You´re sad.   _____

3. She´s happy.   _____

4. It´s cold.   _____

5. They´re angry   _____

Unit 1. My feelings

7. Draw and write. How do you feel?

- -

Unit 1. My feelings

8. Write questions and answer them.

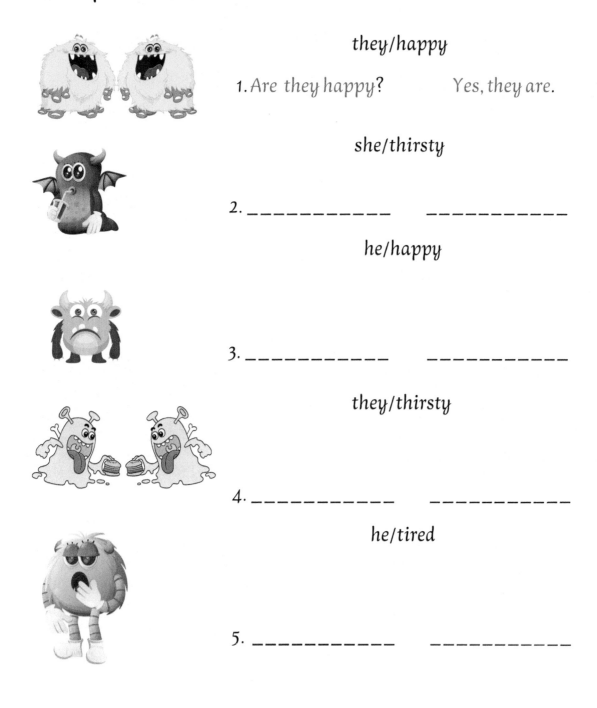

they/happy

1. Are they happy?   Yes, they are.

she/thirsty

2. _____   _____

he/happy

3. _____   _____

they/thirsty

4. _____   _____

he/tired

5. _____   _____

Unit 1. My feelings

Phonics

Letters ai together in a word
long a sound
read and match these words and pictures

sailboat

rainbow

train

rain

paint

snail

Unit 1. My feelings

Reading

The Train

I saw a red train.
A monkey with a small tail said "Wait, wait."
He jumped on the train, as it started to rain.
A snail waited for the train too.
He paid and jumped on the train.

Unit 2. Outdoor toys

Can and Can´t

Can means that you are able to do something. Can´t means you are not able to do something. The form of can doesn´t change. We use it before the base form of other words.

Positive

I can swim

Negative

I can´t/cannot swim

Unit 2. Outdoor toys

1. Tick the right one

She can dance ☐

She can´t dance ☐

He can dance ☐

He can´t dance ☐

He can play football ☐

He can´t play football ☐

She can jumprope ☐

She can´t jumprope ☐

Unit 2. Outdoor toys

2. Write *can* or *can't*

1. We can skateboard,

we _____ play tennis.

2. We ____, play tennis

we _____ play football.

3. We ____, do puzzles

we _____ draw pictures.

4. We ____, do puzzles

we _____ draw pictures.

Unit 2. Outdoor toys

3. Write sentences. Use *can* or *can´t* and the words in the box.

ride a bike   skate   skateboard   play tennis   play football   jump rope

1. She *can´t* play tennis.

2. He _____

3. They _____

4. She _____

5. She _____

6. We _____

Unit 2. Outdoor toys

4. Tick about you.

Action	Can	Can't
write		
ride a bike		
skate		
skateboard		
play tennis		
play football		

Unit 2. Outdoor toys

5. *Draw and write about you.*

Unit 2. Outdoor toys

Can....questions

We use can in yes/no questions to find out what people can do.
We change the word order in yes/no questions.

Statement	Quesrion	Short answers
He can skateboard	Can he skateboard?	Yes, he can / No, he can´t

Unit 2. Outdoor toys

6. Match

A

B

1. Can she skateboard?   _ _

2. Can they play football?   _ _

3. Can you jump rope?   _ _

4. Can he ride a bike?   _ _

C

D

Unit 2. Outdoor toys

7. Make the sentences into questions

1. You can play football.

_____

2. He can skateboard.

_____

3. They can play tennis.

_____

4. She can jump rope.

_____

Unit 2. Outdoor toys

8. Look at the chart. Write the questions and answers.

	Alex	Bella	Cathy
Ride a bike	✔	✔	✔
Skateboard	✔	✗	✗
Play tennis	✗	✔	✗

1. Alex asks Cathy.

Alex; _____ ride a bike? Cathy; _____

2. Bella asks Cathy about Alex

Bella; _____ play tennis? Cathy; _____

3. Cathy asks Alex about Bella

Cathy; _____ skateboard? Alex; _____

4. Alex asks Bella and Cathy

Alex; _____ skateboard? Bella and Cathy; _____

Unit 2. Outdoor toys

Phonics

Letters oa together in a word
long o sound
read and match these words and pictures

coach

oak tree

goat

coat

float

boat

Unit 2. Outdoor toys

Reading

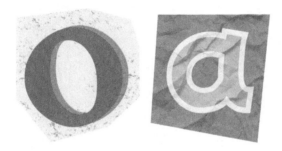

The Old Goat

The old man lives on Oak Street with his old goat.

Today, he will take his goat on a boat. They will float down the river to see the coast. The old goat likes bread, so the old man will feed him a loaf.

Unit 3 Lessons

We and our; they and their

We is a subject pronoun. We use *we* when we talk about two or more people including ourselves.

They is a subject pronoun. We use *they* when we talk about two or more people (not including ourselves)

Our and *their* are possessive adjectives. They say who owns something
we -- our bags, our poster   they -- their bags, their poster.
The other possessive adjective are my, your, his, her and its

Unit 3. Lessons

1. Look and match

	Monday	Tuesday
Class 2	English, maths science	P.E Art
Class 1	P.E Art	English, maths, science

1.   We´ve got maths   on Monday

2. They´ve got maths   on Monday

3. we´ve got art   on Tuesday

4. They´ve got art   on Tuesday

Unit 3. Lessons

2. Look at the picture, write *We´ve got* or
They´ve got

1. *We´ve got* English on Mondays.

2. _____ science on Tuesday.

3. _____ P:E on Tuesday.

4. _____ P:E on Tuesday.

5. _____ science on Tuesday.

6. _____ art on Tuesday.

7. _____ art on Tuesday.

8. _____ English on Tuesday.

Unit 3. Lessons

3. Look and match

Ours

Theirs

4. Write our or their

1. These are their bags

2. These are _ _ _ _ _ _ bags.

3. This is _ _ _ _ _ _ map.

4. These are _ _ _ _ _ _ books.

5. These are _ _ _ _ _ _ books

6. This is _ _ _ _ _ _ map.

Unit 3. Lessons

When have we got....? What have we got....?

What have got ....? and When have we got...? are wh..questions.

We use when to ask about the time something happens. We use what to ask for other information.

On is a preposition of time. We use on before a day of the week to say when somthing happens.

Unit 3. Lessons

5. Look and match

1.When have we got art?

2. What have we got on Wednesday?

3. When have we got English?

4. What have got on Saturday?

English, maths and P.E.

On Monday and Wednesday.

We haven´t got school.

On Tuesday.

Unit 3. Lessons

6. Write what lessons and activities
          you have got.

MONDAY	TUESDAY	WEDNESDAY	THURSDAY	FRIDAY

Unit 3. Lessons

7. Write *What have we got* or *When have we got*.

1. When have we got English?

2. _____ on Tuesday?

3. _____ science?

4. _____ P.E.?

5. _____ on Monday?

8. Write the words in the correct order. Make questions.

1. have we on Monday What got

What have we got on Monday?

2. have When got we P.E

_____

3. got What we have on Tuesday

_____

4. English have got we When

_____

5. When science got have we

_____

6. on Wednesday got What we have

_____

Unit 3. Lessons

Phonics

*Letters ie together in a word
long i sound
read and match these words and pictures*

die

fried

tie

pie

cried

flies

Unit 3. Lessons

Reading

French Fries

Can we have some more friends fries?¨Tom asked his dad.
His dad replied, ¨No Tom you are having a slice of pie for
dessert after your dinner.¨Tom cried and tried again,
¨Please dad!¨. His dad agreed and let him get another order
of fries. ¨This is the best day ever!¨cried Tom.

Unit 4. After School

The present simple
(I do)

We use the present simple of verbs like do, play and help to talk about things we usually do. They are things we do every day, every week or every year.

I play   I help

I do homework   I go swimming

Unit 4. After school

1. Write the day of the week.

Monday

Tuesday

Wednesday

Thursday

1. I help my mum _____
2. I visit my grandma _____
3. I go swimming _____
4. I play piano _____
5. I go to the park _____

Friday

Unit 4. After school

2. Write the verb

| watch | play | go | draw | write | read |

1. I _ _ _ _ _ _ _ TV.

2. I _ _ _ _ _ with friends.

3. I _ _ _ _ _ _ emails.

4. I _ _ _ _ _ _ _ pictures.

5. I _ _ _ _ swimming.

6. I _ _ _ _ _ _ books.

Unit 4. After school

3. Write sentences. Use a verb from the first box and words from the second box

| watch | help | go | listen | do |

| swimming | my homework | to music | TV | my mum |

1. Every Monday

I_____

2. Every Tuesday

I_____

3. Every Wednesday

I_____

4. Every Thursday

I_____

5. Every Friday

I_____

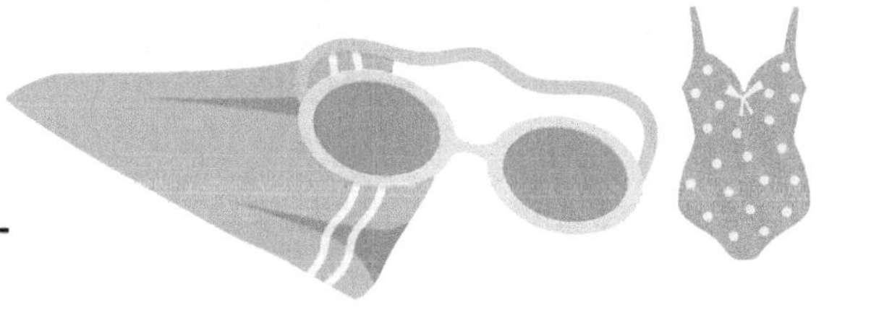

Unit 4. After school

The present simple negative (I don´t do)

After school I don´t play piano.

We use the present simple negative to talk about things we do not usually do

I don´t help my mum
I don´t watch TV   don´t = do not

Unit 4. After school

4. Tick the correct one.

| After school | Monday | Tuesday | Wednesday |

1. Every Monday....

I do my homework ☐
I don't do my homework ☐

2. Every Monday....

I watch TV ☐
I don't watch TV ☐

3. Every Tuesday...

I play football ☐
I don't play football ☐

4. Every Tuesday...

I listen to music ☐
I don't listen to music ☐

5. Every Wednesday

I play football ☐
I don't play football ☐

6. Every Wednesday

I play football ☐
I don't play football ☐

Unit 4. After school

5, Write sentences. Use the present simple
   affirmative and negative.

read books help my mum listen to music   visit my grandma
go swimming play piano do my homework   watch TV

1. I _ _ _ _ _ _ _ _ _ _
I don´t _ _ _ _ _ _ _ _

2. I _ _ _ _ _ _ _ _ _ _
I _ _ _ _ _ _ _ _ _ _ _

3. I _ _ _ _ _ _ _ _ _ _
I _ _ _ _ _ _ _ _ _ _

4. I _ _ _ _ _ _ _ _ _ _
I _ _ _ _ _ _ _ _ _ _

Unit 4. After school

6. Tick and write what you do after school

After school	yes	no
do my homework		
help my mum		
watch TV		
play with friends		
read books		
draw pictures		
Music class		
play tennis		
play football		

1. I do _ _ _ _ _ _ _ _ _ _ _ _ _ _

2. I don´t _ _ _ _ _ _ _ _ _ _ _

3. I _ _ _ _ _ _ _ _ _ _ _ _ _ _

4. I _ _ _ _ _ _ _ _ _ _ _ _ _ _

5, I _ _ _ _ _ _ _ _ _ _ _ _ _ _

6. I _ _ _ _ _ _ _ _ _ _ _ _ _ _

7. I _ _ _ _ _ _ _ _ _ _ _ _ _ _

8. I _ _ _ _ _ _ _ _ _ _ _ _ _ _

9. I _ _ _ _ _ _ _ _ _ _ _ _ _ _

Unit 4. After school

Phonics

Letters ee together in a word
long eee sound
read and match these words and pictures

sneeze

cheese

sheep

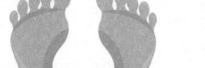

feet

eels

bees

Unit 4. After school

Reading

Lee the Sheep

Lee the sheep couldn't sleep. The birds would cheep, the cars would beep and keep him from sleep. For three weeks, no sleep. He needed to sleep! So he put cheese in each ear to keep out the beeps and the cheeps. Now he is free to sleep for weeks.

Unit 5. Presents

He likes, he doesn´t like

I like sweets   I don´t like chocolate

He likes chocolate   He doesn´t like sweets

she likes nuts   She doesn´t like nuts

When we use he, she and it with the verb like,
we add s. In the negative we use doesn´t

doesn´t = does not

Unit 5. Presents

1. Match

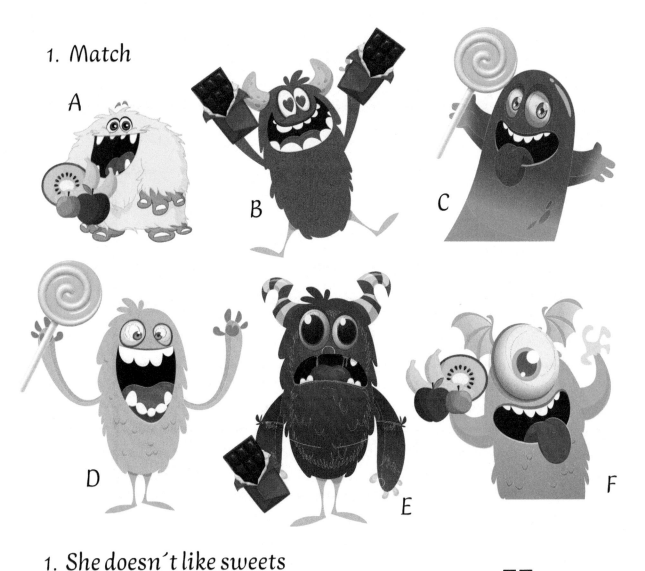

A

B

C

D

E

F

1. She doesn´t like sweets   __

2. He likes fruit   __

3. He doesn´t like fruit   __

4. She likes sweets   __

5. She likes chocolate   __

6. He doesn´t like chocolate   __

Unit 5. Presents

2. Look and write. Who is it?

	Likes	Doesn't like
Ted	sweets	Chocolate
Tina	pears	cakes
Harry	apples	sweets
Holly	cakes	nuts
Sam	nuts	pears

1. She likes pears. She doesn't like cakes   _____

2. He likes nuts. She doesn't like pears   _____

3. He likes sweets. She doesn't like chocolate   _____

4. She likes cakes. She doesn't like nuts   _____

5. He likes apples. She doesn't like sweets   _____

Unit 5. Presents

3. Follow and write sentences. Choose a word from the box.

presents nuts carrots balloons sweets chocolate fruit cakes

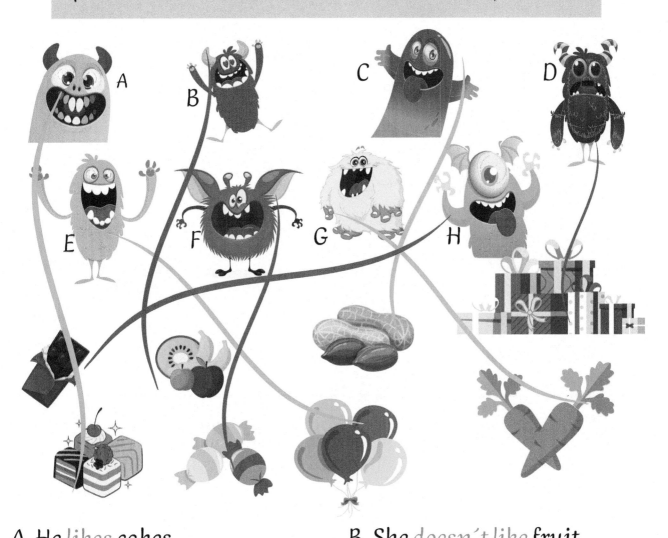

A. He *likes* cakes.

B. She *doesn't like* fruit.

C. She _____.

D. She _____.

E. He _____.

F. He _____.

G. She _____.

H. He _____.

Unit 5. Presents

Questions with like

We use does with like to make questions with he, she and it.

What does he/she like?

Does he/she like....?   Yes, he/she does.

                              No, he/she doesn't

Unit 5. Presents

4. Match

1. What does he like?   No, he doesn´t.

2. What does she like?   He likes cake.

3. Does he like balloons?   She likes fruit

4. Does she like balloons?   Yes, she does.

5. Write the words in the correct order. Make questions.

1. does   like   he   What   2. she   What   like   does

_ _ _ _ _ _ _ _ _ _ _ _ _ _ _   _ _ _ _ _ _ _ _ _ _ _ _ _ _ _

3. she   Does   like   cake   4. like   Do   balloons   you

_ _ _ _ _ _ _ _ _ _ _ _ _ _ _   _ _ _ _ _ _ _ _ _ _ _ _ _ _ _

5. like   she   chocolate   Does   6. Does   fruit   he   like

_ _ _ _ _ _ _ _ _ _ _ _ _ _ _   _ _ _ _ _ _ _ _ _ _ _ _ _ _ _

Unit 5. Presents

5. Draw and write about what you like.

Unit 5. Presents

6. Write questions and answers.

| she | | nuts |

1. What does she like?   She likes nuts.

| he/cakes | | yes |

2. Does he like cakes?   Yes, he does.

| she/sweets | | no |

3. _____?   _____

| he | | presents |

4. _____?   _____

| she/balloons | | yes |

5. _____?   _____

Unit 5. Presents

7. Write answers.

1. Does he like presents?

_____

3. Does she like nuts?

_____

5. Does he like balloons?

_____

2. What does she like?

_____

4. Does he like fruit?

_____

6. Does she like balloons?

_____

Unit 5. Presents

Phonics

Letters or together in a word
long orrr sound
read and match these words and pictures

torn

born

corn

storm

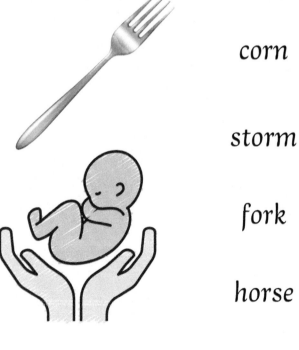

fork

horse

Unit 5. Presents

Reading

Porky

Porky is the pet pig. He is missing. The kids look for Porky everywhere. They look by the fort. Dad brings a torch. What a chore! They can´t find Porky. Then, they hear a snort. It was Porky. Porky was eating corn on the porch.

Unit 6. Every day.

The present simple he/she goes

She has breakfast

She gets up at o´clock

She goes to school at 8 o´clock

We use the present simple talk about things we usually do.
When the pronoun is he, she or it we add s to the verb
When the verb ends in o we add es. The verb have is different

	get up	go	have
He	gets up	goes	has
She	gets up	goes	has
It	gets up	goes	has

Unit 6. Every day

1. True or false T/F

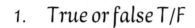

A

B

C

D

A. Max gets up at 6 o´clock   _ _ _ _ _ _ _ _

B. Max goes to school at 9 o´clock   _ _ _ _ _ _ _ _

C. Max gets home at 4 o´clock   _ _ _ _ _ _ _ _

D. Max goes to football at 5 O´clock _ _ _ _ _ _ _ _

Unit 6. Every day

2. Look, match and write.

1. Rex	has breakfast	at 5 o'clock
2. Max	gets up	at 6 o'clock
3. Zack	goes to school	at 9 o'clock
4. Rex	plays football	at 4 o'clock
5. Tina	goes home	at 7 o'clock
6. Zack	goes to bed	at 8 o'clock

Unit 6. Every day

1. Rex   gets up at 6 o´clock

2.   _____

3.   _____

4.   _____

5.   _____

6.   _____

3. Complete the sentences

	get up	have dinner	go to bed
Rex	6	7	9
Tina	7	8	9
Max	7	9	10
Zack	8	6	7

1. Rex gets up at 6 o´clock

2. Tina _____ at 9 o´clock

3. Max _____ at 7 o´clock

4. Zack _____ at 8 o´clock

5. Tina_____ at 8 o´clock

Unit 6. Every day

The present simple negative (he doesn't go)

Tina doesn't get up at 6 o'clock. She gets up at 7 o'clock

We use present simple negative to talk about things we do not usually do. With he, she and it we use doesn't and the verb.

He doesn't go to school
She doesn't have breakfast
It doesn't go to bed.

doesn't = does not

Unit 6. Every day

4. Tick the correct one

He gets up at 7 o´clock

He doesn´t get up at 7 o´clock

He goes to football at 5 o´clock

He doesn´t go to football at 5 o´clock

She has breakfast at 8 o´clock

she doesn´t have breakfast at 8 o´clock

He goes to school at 8 o´clock

He doesn´t go to 8 at o´clock

Unit 6. Every day

5. Write about you. Answer the questions

What time do you get up?

_____

What time do you have breakfast?

_____

What time do you go to school?

_____

What time do you go to home?

_____

What time do you go to
football/tennis/basketball?

_____

What time do you have dinner?

_____

What time do you go to bed?

_____

Unit 6. Every day

6. Make the sentences negative.

1. He gets up at 6 o´clock.

    He doesn't get up at 6 o´clock

2. She goes to school at 8 o´clock.

_____

3. He has dinner at 9 o´clock.

_____

4. She goes to bed at 7 o´clock.

_____

5. She goes home at 4 o´clock.

_____

6. He goes to bed at 9 o´clock.

_____

Unit 6. Every day

7. make the information correct.

	get up	have dinner	go to bed
Rex	6	7	9
Tina	7	8	9
Max	7	9	10
Zack	8	6	7

1. Rex gets up at 7 o´clock.

He doesn´t get up at 7 o´clock. He gets up at 6 o´clock

2. Tina gets up at 8 o´clock

She _ _ _ _ _ _ _ _ _ _ 8 o´clock. She _ _ _ _ _ _ _ _ at 7 o´clock

3. Max has dinner at 8 o´clock.

He _ _ _ _ _ _ _ _ _ _ 8 o´clock. He _ _ _ _ _ _ _ _ at 9 o´clock

4. Zack goes to be at 8 o´clock.

He _ _ _ _ _ _ _ _ _ _ 8 o´clock. He _ _ _ _ _ _ _ _ at 7 o´clock

Unit 6. Every day

Phonics

Letters zz together in a word
long zzzzz sound
read and match these words and pictures

Sizzle

Pizza

Puzzle

Buzz

Fizzy

Fuzz

Unit 6. Every day

Reading

Zoey and Zach

Zoey and Zach went on a field trip to the zoo. When they got there, it was windy with some drizzle. Zoey zipped her jacket. "Come on" said Zach "Let's go see the new buzzing bees! The exhibit is right next to the zebras!"
Zoey could hear the bees buzzing (zzzzzz) Zoey and Zach ran in a zig-zag! They were buzzing like the bees. Later Zoey and Zach had pizza and a fizzy drink.

Unit 7. Places.

Where does he work?

Where does he work? is a wh question. We use where to as about a place. We use a does to make questions with he, she and it in the present simple. The word order changes in questions.

Statement	Questions
He works...	Where does he work?
She works....	Where does she work?
It works...	Where does it work?

Remember the s on the end of the verb with he, she and it in statements in the present simple.

Unit 7. Places

1. Match

1. Where does she work?

She works in a zoo.

2. Where does he work?

She works in a school.

3. Where does she work?

He works in a supermarket.

4. Where does she work?

She works in a hospital.

5. Where does he work?

He works in a fire station.

Unit 7. Places

Does he work...? Yes, he does/No, he doesn´t.

Does he work ...? is a yes/no question. We can
answer Yes, he does or No, he doesn´t .

Question	Short answers
Does he work...?	Yes, he does/No, he doesn´t.
Does she work...?	Yes, she does/No, she doesn´t.
Does it work...?	Yes, it does/No it doesn´t.

Unit 7. Places

2. *Answer the questions.*

1. *Where does she work?*

   Does she work in an office?

———————————————

———————————————

2. *Where does he work?*

   Does he work in a shop?

——————————

——————————

Unit 7. Places

3

3. Where does he work?

Does she work in a school?

_____

_____

4

4. Where does he work?

Does he work in a zool?

_____

_____

5

5. Where does he work?

Does he work in a bank?

_____

_____

Unit 7. Places

Prepositions of time

Jamie goes to school in the morning. On Monday he has English

In the afternoon he goes swimming

He does his homework in the evening

He goes to bed at 9 o ´clock at night

On, in and at are prepositions of time
We use on with the days of the week
We use in with the morning, afternoon and evening
We use at with times of the day and night
We use when to ask questions about time
When does he go to school? At 8 o´clock in the morning

Morning = until lunch

Afternoon = after lunch before dinner

evening = after dinner before bed

Night = when its dark and time for bed

Unit 7. Places

3. Circle the correct word

1. He goes home in/on the afternoon.

2. She has science on/at Monday.

3. It sleeps in/at night.

4. He has dinner at/in 7 o´clock

5. She watches TV on/in the evening

6. He has breakfast on/at 7 o´clock

4. Write in, on or at

1. in the morning

2. _ _ _ _ _ _ _ the afternoon.

3. _ _ _ _ _ _ night.

4. _ _ _ _ _ _ Tuesday.

5. _ _ _ _ _ _ 3 o´clock.

6. _ _ _ _ _ _ the evening

7. _ _ _ _ _ Friday.

8. _ _ _ _ _ 7 o´clock

Unit 7. Places

5. Make questions about Jamie and answer them.

1. go to school/in the morning

Does he go to school in the morning?   Yes, he does

2. when/do his homework

‗‗‗‗‗‗‗‗‗‗‗‗‗‗‗‗‗‗‗‗‗‗‗‗   ‗‗‗‗‗‗‗‗‗‗‗‗

3. watch TV/in the morning

‗‗‗‗‗‗‗‗‗‗‗‗‗‗‗‗‗‗‗‗‗‗‗‗   ‗‗‗‗‗‗‗‗‗‗‗‗

4. when/go to bed

‗‗‗‗‗‗‗‗‗‗‗‗‗‗‗‗‗‗‗‗‗‗‗‗   ‗‗‗‗‗‗‗‗‗‗‗‗

5. go swimming/in the morning

‗‗‗‗‗‗‗‗‗‗‗‗‗‗‗‗‗‗‗‗‗‗‗‗   ‗‗‗‗‗‗‗‗‗‗‗‗

Unit 7. Places

6. do his homework/at night

----------------------------- - - - - - - - - - -

7. when/have science

----------------------------- - - - - - - - - - -

8. do his homework/in the evening

----------------------------- - - - - - - - - - -

9. when/go to school

----------------------------- - - - - - - - - - -

10. when/go swimming

----------------------------- - - - - - - - - - -

Unit 7. Places

Phonics

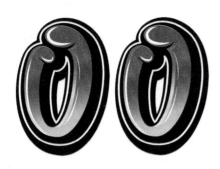

Letters oo together in a word
long ooooo sound and short o sound
read and match these words and pictures

long ooooo

wood

broom

hood

moon

book

spoon

cook

baboon

short o

Unit 7. Places

Reading long ooo

My Scooter

My dad got me a new scooter for my birthday. He picked out a blue one. I ride my scooter to school everyday. At first, I felt goofy, I had no clue how to ride one. Then, I practised some more. Now I can ride smooth. A group of kids in my neighbourhood ride together in the afternoon. I love my blue scooter.

Reading short o

Good Book

"What a good book!" said Will. The book was about a cook who was a crook and he took some wood to brook to make a dam. He had a hood made of wood and book that he shook when he stood. At the brook some soot fell on his foot. "Oh look" said a rook, "I can see a cook who is a crook down by the brook and he has soot on his foot! That's not very good!"

Unit 8. Weather

What's the weather like? It's....

What's the weather like? is a wh-question. We use it to find out about the weather. We answer with It's

what's = what is

it's = it is

Unit 8. The weather

1. Match the pictures

1. It´s raining. ___   2. It´s hot. ___

3. It´s snowing. ___   4. It´s cold. ___

5. It´s windy. ___   6. It´s sunny. ___

Unit 8. The weather

2. What's the weather like?

1. It's snowing

2. _____

3. _____

4. _____

5. _____

6. _____

Unit 8. The weather

3. What weather do you like? Write and draw.

Unit 8. The weather

Imperatives

Put on is an imperative. We use imperatives to tell somebody what to do. The imperative for is the same as the base form of the verb.

Don't put on is a negative imperative. We use negative imperatives to tell somebody not to do something.

Unit 8. The weather

4. Match.

1. It´s cold.	__	a. Don´t put on your coat.
2. It´s windy.	__	b. Fly a kite.
3. It´s hot.	__	c. Make a snowman.
4. It´s raining.	__	d. Don´t forget your umbrella.
5. It´s snowing.	__	e. Wear a sun hat.
6. It´s sunny.	__	f. Wear a coat.

5. Unscramble and write

1. the What´s like weather

What´s the weather like?

2. your Put coat on.

_____

3. raining It´s

4. hat on put Don´t your

_____ _____

5. it sunny Is

6. is it Yes,

_____ _____

Unit 8. The weather

Punctuation

Dear Jon

My name's Jamie. I'm in class 2. My sister's name is Alison. My friends are Dave, Angie and Emma. I like English and PE. What do you like?
Write to me soon!
From Jamie

When we write a sentence, we begin with a capital letter and end with a full stop. Names also begin with a capital letter.

We use an apostrophe for short form and to show possession.

We use a comma in a sentence to show where to stop for a short time, when there is a list of words, for example.

We use a question mark at the end of questions.

We sometimes use an exclamation mark at the end of a sentence with an imperative

Unit 8. The weather

6. Match the punctuations.

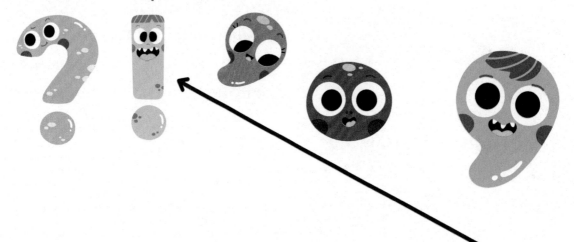

full stop   apostrophe   question mark   exclamation mark

7. Circle the punctuation.

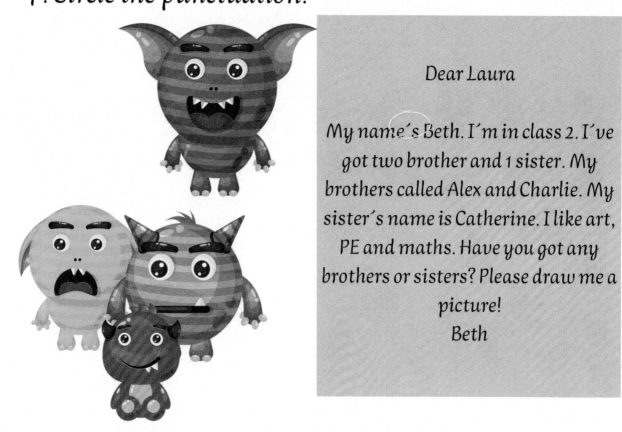

Dear Laura

My name's Beth. I'm in class 2. I've got two brother and 1 sister. My brothers called Alex and Charlie. My sister's name is Catherine. I like art, PE and maths. Have you got any brothers or sisters? Please draw me a picture!
Beth

Unit 8. The weather

8. Add the punctuation.

Unit 8. The weather

This is my house. My bedroom is upstairs next to the bathroom My living room is above my bedroom The kitchen is downstairs next to the hallway We have a garden with lots of flowers Have you got a garden Draw your house and write about it

Unit 8. The weather

9. Draw your house and write about it.

Unit 8. The weather

Phonics

Letters ch together in a word
make the sound ch
read and match these words and pictures

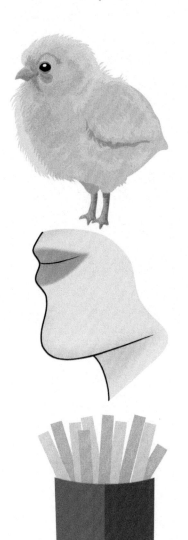

lunch

chips

cheese

chick

chain

chin

Unit 8. The weather

Reading

Chad and the Chimp
Chad is on his way home when
he sees a chimp. Chad rubs his
chin as he looks at the chimp.
The chimp eats a cherry as it
looks at Chad. The chimp sees
two yellow chicks pass by and
runs after them.

Unit 9. On the Farm

Comparative adjectives.

Big and loud are adjectives. Adjectives describe things or people. Bigger and louder are comparative adjectives. We use comparative adjectives to describe the difference between two things or people. we make the comparative by adding er to the end of the adjective.

small - smaller   loud - louder   quiet - quieter

fast - faster   slow - slower

We use this and these to talk about people and things that are near us. We use that and those to talk about people and things that are far from us.

Unit 9. On the farm

1. Circle the comparative adjectives

The horse is big. The cow is bigger.
The horse is quiet. The cow is quieter

The hen is loud. The goose is louder.
The donkey is slow. The cow is slower

The sheep is small. The hen is smaller.
The cow is fast. The goat is faster.

2. Choose a or b

This cow is bigger ___   This pig is fatter ___

This sheep is older ___   This chick is younger

Unit 9. On the farm

3. Complete the sentences. Use
   the adjectives in brackets.

1. The goose is bigger (big)

2. The _ _ _ _ is _ _ _ _ (slow)

3. The _ _ _ _ is _ _ _ _ (small)

4. The _ _ _ _ is _ _ _ _ (fast)

5. The _ _ _ _ is _ _ _ _ (tall)

6. The _ _ _ _ is _ _ _ _ (loud)

Unit 9. On the farm

Comparatives with *than*

We use than after a comparative adjective
when we compare one thing directly with
another
The donkey is smaller than the horse.
Dad is older than mum

Unit 9. On the farm

4. Tick the correct one

Ann is older than Lily __

Ann is younger than Lily __

Lily is older than Bob __

Bob is older than Lily __

Lily is shorter than Ann __

Ann is taller than Lily __

Bob is shorter than Lily __

Lily is taller than Bob __

5. Write sentences.

Bob/young/Ann

1. Bob is younger than Ann.

Ann/short/Lily

2._____

Bob/small/Lily

3._____

Lily/tall/Bob

4._____

Lily/old/Ann

4._____

Lily/big/Ann

4._____

Unit 9. On the farm

The conjunction and

The horse is big, It's bigger than the donkey and it's bigger than the sheep

Lily is bigger than Ann and she's louder than Ann

And is a conjunction (a linking word). We use it to join two sentences together to make one sentence

The horse is bigger than the goat. The goat is bigger than the chicken

The horse is bigger than the goat and the goat is bigger than the chicken

In the sentence we remove the full stop, add and then change the capital T with a lowercase t

Unit 9. On the farm

6. Write and join the sentences.

1. The cow is bigger than the goat. The goat is bigger than the goose

The cow is bigger than the goat *and the goat is bigger than the goose.*

2. Ann is younger than Lily. Bob is younger than Ann

Ann is younger than Lily _ _ _ _ _ _ _ _ _ _ _ _ _ _ _ _ _ _ _

3. Open the window. Close the door

Open the window _

4. She's a doctor. He's a policeman

She's a doctor _

5. She works in a hospital. He works in a police station.

She works in a hospital _

6. Wash your face. Brush your teeth.

Wash your face _

Unit 9. On the farm

Phonics

Letters sh together in a word
make the sound shhh
read and match these words and pictures

shark

shirt

paint brush

shoes

sheep

fish

Unit 9. On the farm

Shelly´s Day

On Sunday, Shelly went to the beach. There was a shark in the ocean, so she couldn't go swimming. Shelly looked for shells in the sand and played with her toy ship. She also dug a hole with her shovel. Next, she sat in the shade and ate an ice cream from the shop. Shelly had shower when she go home.

Unit 10. In school

Quantifiers (some any)
ordinal numbers
The past simple of be
irregular plural nouns

Some and any

we use some and any to talk about more than one thing or person when we do not say the exact number.

We use some in a positive sentences and any in negative sentences

Unit 10. In school

1 Circle A or B

There are some chairs   A B

There aren´t any   A B
students

There are some   A B
teachers

There aren´t any   A B
chairs

There are some tables   A B

There aren´t any   A B
students

There aren´t any   A B
teachers

There are some   A B
lockers

There aren´t any   A B
tables

Unit 10. In school

2. Write some or any

There aren't _ _ _ _ children   There are _ _ _ _ teachers

There are _ _ _ _ drinks   There aren't _ _ _ _ computers

There aren't _ _ _ _ teachers   There are _ _ _ _ computers

There are _ _ _ _ students   There aren't _ _ _ _ drinks

Unit 10. In school

3. Make the sentences negative

There are some children.   There aren't any children

There are some pictures.   _____

There are some teachers   _____

There are some chairs   _____

There are some posters   _____

4. Make the sentences positive.

There aren't any cars   There are some cars.

There aren't any cupboards   _____

There aren't any prizes   _____

There aren't any pegs   _____

There aren't any tables   _____

Unit 10. In school

Ordinal numbers

First, second and third are ordinal numbers. We can us them to talk about the order things or people are in, for example in a competition or a race.

Cardinal	Ordinal	Cardinal	Ordinal
one 1	first 1st	six 6	sixth 6th
two 2	second 2nd	seven 7	seventh 7th
three 3	third 3rd	eight 8	eighth 8th
four 4	fourth 4th	nine 9	ninth 9th
five 5	fifth 5th	ten 10	tenth 10th

Unit 10. In school

5. Write the ordinal numbers.

I was at the school open day yesterday. There was an English competition. The winner of the *first* prize was Tina. The winner of the _ _ _ _ _ _ _ prize was Dave, and the winner of the _ _ _ _ _ _ _ prize was Joey.

6. Write the ordinal numbers.

Red   Shorty   Jenny   Max   Tina   Jack

Jack is *first*   Tina is _ _ _ _ _ _

Max is _ _ _ _ _ _   Jenny is _ _ _ _ _ _

Shorty is _ _ _ _ _ _   Red is _ _ _ _ _ _

Unit 10. In school

Was and were

Jamie's tired. Yesterday he was the superhero in the school play

Mum and dad were happy.

Was and were are the past simple forms of the verb be. We use the past simple of be with adjectives to describe feelings in the past.

Today (Tuesday)
I am hot
Jamie is tired
Mum and dad are happy

Yesterday (Monday)
I was cold
Jamie was happy
Mum and dad were happy

We also use the past simple of be to identify someone or something in the past, to talk about the location of someone or something in the past and to talk about the time and weather in the past.

Unit 10. In school

7. Circle the past simple forms of *be*.

Yesterday I (was) at the park. My friends were at the park. It was windy. There was a girl with a kite. The kite was in the tree. The girl was sad. There was a tall lady. She helped and then the kite was in the sky and we were all happy.

8. Where were the yesterday? look and write.

1. *She was at the zoo.*

2. They _____

3. She _____

4. They _____

Unit 10. In school

Wasn't and weren't

The negative forms of was and were are was not and were not. We usually use the short forms wasn't and weren't

Affirmative	Negative
I was	I wasn't
you/we/they were	you/we/they weren't
he/she/it was	he/she/it wasn't

9. Circle the correct past simple negative form of be.

1. Mum and dad wasn't / weren't sad.

2. Tina wasn't / weren't good.

3. Jamie wasn't / weren't a policeman.

4. It wasn't / weren't sunny yesterday.

5. We wasn't / weren't in the living room.

6. They wasn't / weren't in the park.

Unit 10. In school

Plural nouns

We use the plural form when we are talking about more than one thing or person. We add s

one boy   two boys   Some plural nouns are different. They are irregular plurals

Singular	Plural
one lolly	two lollies
one family	two families
one tomato	three tomatoes
one sandwich	three sandwiches
one shelf	four shelves

one child   two children

one woman   two women

one man   two men

Unit 10. In school

10. Circle the regular plurals and underline the irregular plurals

1. There's a monkey! I like monkeys.

2. Jamie's got a big family. Tony and Martin have got small families.

3. Alison is eating a pastry. She likes pastries.

4. Ann's playing with a toy. On Saturdays she plays with her toys.

5. There's a sandwich in my lunchbox. I like sandwiches.

6. Is there a shelf? Yes, in the room there are four shelves.

11. Complete the table

singular	Shelf		Party		Lolly
plural		Pastries		families	

Unit 10. In school

Phonics

Letters th together in a word make the sounds th voice (the) and th voiceless (three)

read and match these words and pictures

Thirty

Weather

Mother

Moth

Father

Thumb

Unit 10. In school

Reading

My brother, Arthur is the weatherman. He wanted to tell everyone about the weather in the. First, he said there was a blizzard in North America. It was cold for everyone. They had over thirteen inches of snow on the ground! The kids were off school for thirty days! They wanted to make a snowman. Next, he said that it would be very hot in South America. The people here wanted to go in the ocean to cool off. Then they wanted to play tetherball on the beach. They all enjoyed playing the weather! My brother is happy he is the weatherman,

Review

Grammar reference
Have got

Affirmative Short form	Affirmative Long form	Negative Short form	Negative Long form
I´ve got	I have got	I haven´t got	I have not got
you´ve got	you have got	you haven´t got	you have not got
he´s got	he has got	he hasn´t got	he has not got
she´s got	she has got	she hasn´t got	she has not got
it´s got	it has got	it hasn´t got	it has not got
we´ve got	we have got	we haven´t got	we have not got
you´ve got	you have got	you haven´t got	you have not got
they´ve got	they have got	they haven´t got	they have not got

Questions	Short answers	Negative
have I got?	Yes, I have.	No, I haven´t.
have you got?	Yes, you have.	No, you haven´t
has he got?	Yes, he has.	No, he hasn´t.
has she got?	Yes, she has.	No, she hasn´t
has it got?	Yes, it has.	No, it hasn´t.
have we got?	Yes, we have	No, we haven´t.
have you got?	Yes, you have.	No, you haven´t
have they got?	Yes, they have.	No, they haven´t.

Grammar reference

Be (Present simple)

Affirmative Short form	Affirmative Long form	Negative Short form	Negative Long form
I´m	I am	I´m not	I am not
you´re	you are	you aren't	you are not
he´s	he is	he isn´t	he is not
she´s	she is	she isn´t	she is not
it´s	it is	it isn´t	it is not
we´re	we are	we aren´t	we are not
you´re	you are	you aren´t	you are not
they´re	they are	they aren´t	they are not

Questions	Short answers	Negative
am I?	Yes, I am	No, I´m not
are you?	Yes, you are	No, you aren´t
is he?	Yes, he is	No, he isn´t
is she?	Yes, she is	No, she isn´t
is it?	Yes, it is	No, it isn´t
are we?	Yes, we are	No, we aren´t
are you?	Yes, you are	No, you aren´t
are they?	Yes, they are.	No, they aren´t.

Grammar reference

Can / Can´t

Affirmative Short form	Negative Short form	Negative Long form
I can	I can´t	I cannot
you can	you can´t	you cannot
he can	he can´t	he cannot
she can	she can´t	she cannot
it can	it can´t	it cannot
we can	we can´t	we cannot
you can	you can´t	you cannot
they can	they can´t	they cannot

Questions	Short answers	Negative
Can I?	Yes, I can	No, I can´t
Can you?	Yes, you can	No, you can´t
Can he?	Yes, he can	No, he can´t
Can she?	Yes, she can	No, she can´t
Can it?	Yes, it can	No, it can´t
Can we?	Yes, we can	No, we can´t
Can you?	Yes, you can	No, you can´t
Can they?	Yes, they can	No, they can´t

Grammar reference

Be (Past simple)

Affirmative	Negative Short form	Negative Long form
I was	I wasn´t	I was not
you were	you weren´t	you were not
he was	he wasn´t	he was not
she was	she wasn´t	she wasn´t
it was	it wasn´t	it was not
we were	we weren´t	we were not
you were	you weren´t	you were not
they were	they weren´t	they were not

Questions	Short answers	Negative
was I?	Yes, I was	No, I wasn´t
were you?	Yes, you were	No, you weren´t
was he?	Yes, he was	No, he wasn´t
was she?	Yes, she was	No, she wasn´t
was it?	Yes, it was	No, it wasn´t
were we?	Yes, we were	No, we weren´t
were you?	Yes, you were	No, you weren´t
were they?	Yes, they were	No, they weren´t

Grammar reference

Irregular Plurals

one lolly	two lollies
one family	two families
one pastry	two pastries
one tomato	two tomatoes
one party	two parties
one sandwich	two sandwiches
one shelf	two shelves
one child	two childre
one woman	two women
one man	two men

Printed in Great Britain
by Amazon

29839787R00071